Presentation by *BookLeaf Publishing*

Web: www.bookleafpub.com

E-mail: info@bookleafpub.com

ISBN: 9789357446846

First edition 2022

DEDICATION

Dedicated to the broken dream kids, the people who abandon their aspirations and often reminisce the "What if?"

PREFACE

Jackalope Season means a period of inspiration and creation. Everything goes right for once. Trying something for the first time and doing a good job, yet everyone around you thinks you've been doing this your whole life.

 I submitted these poems as part of challenge where I had to write 21 poems in 21 days. Though to tell you the truth, most of these were written in the final 5 days. These poems come from ideas I had late at night while staring at the ceiling for hours. I've always wanted to publish my own book ever since I was little; and I'm proud I can look back and tell my younger self that I finally did it.

1;11

it's my 18th birthday today

and i can't help but think that i'm not supposed to
be alive

-rethinking things

In another life

we were still friends

i didn't get anxious all the time

i learned how to forgive myself

math was my strong subject

you weren't such a bitch to me

i actually went to sleep at a reasonable time

he apologized.

in another life

everything would be different

and maybe that's the way i want it

PE = mgh

how long does it take for something with
potential energy

to turn into wasted potential?

what if i've already reached that point?

-waiting for an opportunity

the game of life

my dad always said to me

"you never know the value of something till it's
gone"

i thought he meant toy trains or cars

now i know the importance of saying "i love
you"

one too many times

taking photos at every rest stop

so someone knows your journey

making sure your handwriting in a birthday card
is perfect

just in case someone wants to get it tattooed

for nothing in life is permanent

and no one knows where they are in the game of
life

till someone says

"checkmate"

-you promised you'd teach me how to play
chess, you never did

30 feet

i bought my dog a 30 foot long leash today

and it reminded me

that humans would rather have the longest rope
in the world

securing them to safety

than taking the dog off leash

and letting go.

-my dog knows his name, do you know yours?

learning curve

you wore the same shirt i gave you tonight, but why?

was it to make a statement even though our eyes never met?

or was it because you were rushing last minute to get ready, like you always do?

i can't see fucking Prius's the same after you inherited yours fromyour grandparents

nor can i look at our old lunch spot, remembering that sometimes my mom would pack you a lunch herself

watching you dance so freely tonight, i know that was just you being controlled by a puppeteer

or maybe you've finally learned how to let go;

something i never thought you would learn.

corruptio optimi pessima

corruptio optimi pessima

i often worry if what i'm doing is enough

i think back to my classmates in grade school

comparing myself to them and their successes

it's funny, i used to always think this one guy
was so smart

as one of the top students in our small school

you might even say i looked up to him.

it's been 8 years since i last saw him

 now he's selling drugs and living out of his car

while other classmates are in university or
starting their own business

i sit here looking at the evidence photo of an
attempted robbery

corruption of the best is life's worst tragedy

-what happened to Stanford?

indica

smooth milk being poured into a glass

being small in the car, fighting to keep your eyes
open

that moment right before you fall asleep

the hot tub on a summer night

warm clothes fresh out of the dryer

morning dew on blades of grass

the smell of a campfire

watching cartoons

music becomes whole

a weighted blanket

everything is okay

sativa

the thrill of tag during recess

that stage of innocence where everything is
funny

going trick or treating as a kid

everything is entertaining

euphoric

warm pancakes with syrup

looking at the most beautiful night sky

opening presents on x-mas morning

getting lost in thought

time moves at an interesting pace

what was i saying again?

creation?

sometimes i wonder why man created religion

was it really to unify and heal?

or was it just an excuse to create unnecessary
conflicts

with no resolution,

since what you are fighting over

does not exist?

for if a god were to exist,

he would see the useless fighting

and condemn it

for there is no winner in war.

when humans destroy each other in useless
fighting,

it is not called murder

its called a casualty.

because it is expected that in war, in useless
fighting

the resolution is death.

and that is our "solution"

transition(s)

small, patchy forests have started to grow on the
east and west side of the plateau

the mountain that once protruded out has been
leveled

reduced to nothing but a flat plane

yet a deep and thick line now divides it in half

the winds, which used to sound like the cries of
the hawk

now sound as deep as the bears grumble

barely recognizable, as nature is ever
transforming

adapting to new changes along the way

even with a different name

it's still the same land as before

just in a different stage of it's evolution

unsinkable

when anyone asks me what my favorite year is, i
used to always reply

"7th grade"

"unbreakable" bonds were made, and memories
that play on repeat fill my head anytime i hear
the number 7

the titanic and 7th grade have about as much in
common as you and me, but share one similar
thing;

we both believed we were invincible

little did i know that the answer 7th grade was
just a facade-

a facade to cover up a decaying, old and
abandoned building
that i call home.

the same people whomst i trusted with building
me, who steered me through the roughest seas,
across the globe

were inevitably the same ones who led me
down the wrong course-

into an iceberg.

night sky3

it's 3:19 in the morning

and I don't know what hurts more,

the thought of never seeing you again

or the thought of forgetting everything.

-reminisce

seeds of doubt

paralyzed

my hands sit frozen over the glowing light of my
keyboard

emitting from under my blanket

"what ifs" flood my mind

too scared to make another move

until

an idea lurks by

i race to type it out

before doubt plagues my mind

and wins.

-writer's block

sirens

the familiar screeching noise

breaks through the air

move aside, move aside

the sea parts and a transport leads the way

as i see the strobe in my rear view

i can't help but wonder if

a life emerges

or simply disappears

as this fragile thing we call

"life"

rests on a knife's edge

whine

the smell of it on your breath alone is enough to
make me want to slap that mindless grin off your
face

my earliest memories- helping your limp body
up the stairs and into bed

"daddy what's wrong with mom?"

"she's just tired."

too naive to know, too young to comprehend

but i remember it all

every fucking bottle

-earliest memory

education system

i've never liked school

always would dread having to go back in the
morning

never learning, only memorizing

why punish kids when their lack of
understanding is your own fault?

math, science, language arts take priority

arts and electives don't matter anyways

"they won't get you a degree"

no one wants to be there

miserable people who just want to get on with
their lives

on the other hand, kids who don't want to grow
up

only teaching from one point of view

how many more years of this shit do i have left?

when it comes down
to it

i hope you're okay

i got into a college 6 hours away

i bet you hardly even think of me while you go
about your day

so many memories together

yet that all goes down the drain

when it comes down to it

you were the fucking hypocrite

but what does it even matter?

you were the one who taught me best-

you can't please em' all

the lookout

overlooking 580

cars going west, cars going east

feeling so disconnected from reality

seeing shooting stars

virginities lost

memories made

watching fireworks

getting stupidly high and stumbling back to the
house

you feel like a god there

watching everyone go about their day

and you just watch from above

wondering what each person's life is like

perhaps more imperfect than meets the eye.

all you can do is watch,

and just exist for a minute in blissful innocence.

-a bench that only exists in Google Earth now

fin

when people remember me, i don't want them to
pity me

i want to be known

for people to hear my name and know who i was

i know i have a purpose here on earth

but i don't know what it is

they say you die twice

once when you're already in the grave

the second time is the last time someone
mentions your name

who's the most immortal of us all?

-i wasn't born at 1;11 for nothing

4:27

it's an average evening tonight

and i can't help but think that i just need to get
some sleep

-nothing left to rethink